Liberian
Cultures
and
Marriages

Myra Sampson Reeves

Order this book online at www.trafford.com
or email orders@trafford.com

Most Trafford titles are also available at major online book retailers.

Print information available on the last page.

ISBN: 978-1-4269-1179-8 (sc)

Trafford rev. 09/21/2022

www.trafford.com

North America & international
toll-free: 844-688-6899 (USA & Canada)
fax: 812 355 4082

Contents

As a professional counselor, I would like to thank the Philadelphia Board of Education for my primary education. I would like to also thank my secondary institutions Bennett College, University of North Carolina at Greensboro, University of the District of Columbia, George Washington University, University of Pennsylvania, and Wesley Theological Seminary.

I would also like to thank the Christian Stronghold Baptist Church and the Christian Research & Development Training in Biblical Counseling. I am very thankful for the loving support of my church family at the Shiloh Baptist Church, which has been a solid rock in a weary land. Thank you, Mrs. Muriel Gregory and family, and Minister Thelma Pugh and Reverend Desiree Grogan. A special thank you to our pastor, Reverend Wallace Charles Smith and Mrs. Smith.

As a mother, I would like to thank my mother, Emma Sampson for giving birth to me, and my father, Fred O. Sampson, and having the years of discipline & wisdom that you have shared and given. I would also like to thank my Godparents. I would also like to acknowledge my siblings: Eric Sampson and Joanna Sampson for their moral support in my work, education, and their families. Extended family, cousins, nieces, nephews, and a special tribute to the members of the Simmons and Sampson Family reunions; Thank you for instilling in me the heritage of family. I would also like to acknowledge my friends within my childhood, community, and college and family years.

I would also humbly like to acknowledge my mentors: Professor Beth Norcross, Mrs. Sabrina Black, Mrs. Marian Elderman Wright, Mrs. Christina Clark, Mr. Ron Klein, Mrs. Marva Washington, Dr. Michael Kopell, Reverend Jacqueline Thompson, Dr. Crystal Kukendall and Reverend Robert Felton, Girl Scouts of the Nation's Capital, Friends of Liberia and the Liberian Embassy. I would also like to thank my mentors Dr. Carolyn Cousin and Mrs. Carvella Beavers.

I would like to thank the following libraries:

Philadelphia, Fayetteville, N.C. and Prince William County Library in Manassas, VA for the assistance in resources and references. A special thank you to my sister-in-law Cynthia Avery, Satia Nemah, and Melvine Avery for their moral support and encouragement in completing my book. Special recognition to the Pastor of the the White Rock Baptist Church; Reverend William Shaw and my church family. I would also like to acknowledge the Avery, Reeves, and Grace families.

This book will inspire and prepare those that are planning or contemplating marrying into the Liberian Culture and will educate you on the lifestyle of the Liberians in Africa, the Caribbean Islands, Europe, and the United States.

Tribes

Liberia is composed of several ethnic groups, which are composed of 95% African tribes (Kpelle, Bassa, Gio, Kru, Grebo, Mano, Krahn, Gola Gbandi, Loma Kissi, Vai, Dei, Bella, Mandingo, and Mende). There exists 2.5% Americo-Liberians descendants of immigrants from the U.S.A 2.5% descendants of immigrants from the Caribbean who have been slaves. The dominant religions in Liberia are Christians, indigenous beliefs 40%, and Muslim 20%. The official language of the land is English 20% as well as 20 ethnic group languages.

Family Bonds

The families of Liberians are the core component of growth and development in the country. The Family is composed of the nucleus: Husband, who serves as the Head of the family, the wife that serves as the mother and servant to the husband. The children are valued as the jewels in the family to grow and continue the values with in the family. The extended families consist of the grandfather, grandmother, aunts, uncles, nieces, nephews, and cousins. The family provides the guidance for the children to develop spiritually, culturally, and emotionally. The children are taught at a very early age to respect their elders. The elders are any older member in their community. The elders are considered to have the wisdom to teach the children in the village social skills, communication skills, and daily living skills. The culture teaches the young children in the village to respect their family property as well as their neighbor. Once the children have acquired these skills, it is reinforced within their villages, churches, and communities. Many tribal families share what their families acquire, but it is a mutual agreement written or verbal consent between the two or multiple families. An awareness of culture, respect, and ethics are instilled early on with the children before they become adults or parents themselves.

The union of marriages with Afro-American women uniting with Liberian men is growing in the United States. Many Liberians are migrating to the United States and United Kingdom. Many Liberians reside in Europe with their mates. Many Liberians have migrated to various states such as New York, Maine, Pennsylvania, Maryland, New Jersey, California, Utah, Hawaii, North Carolina, South Carolina, Tennessee, Rhode Island, Delaware, Florida, and Minnesota, as well as Washington, D.C.

The cultural diversity between each culture is an adjustment for both persons. Beginning with the food, various dishes consist of: Jalif Rice, which consists of mixed vegetables, chicken, beef, and goat mixed into the rice, Cassava leaves,(a green leaf vegetable that is grown in West Africa) is stewed with pork, beef, chicken, and dry fish. This dish is served over a bed of rice.

Foo-Foo-and Soup is another delicacy, which consists of plantain flour that is molded into a ball and soup, which consists of chicken, beef, pork, fish and pepper served together. These dishes are often served during family traditions such as: weddings, Christenings, birthdays, Christmas, Independence Day, and other special gatherings. The tribal relations of matrimonies are formulated between friends and neighbors. One family may have a daughter, and the other family friend have a son that are paired as children, teenagers, or young adults. The families will exchange food, jewelry, monies, and heirlooms. A mutual exchange if their personal belongings is seen as a "blessing" from God to promote a happy and prosperous marriage to their beloved children.

West African Vegetables, grounded in the yard Pulve Leaves, Egg Plant, Cucumbers, tomatoes, corn, bitter leave, and Cassava Leaves

The Gardening And preparation consist of 2 months to 5 months to Blessing

Lesson on picking palava leaves in the
garden, leaves are either freshly washed
shreded and packed in storage bag.
and place in the Freezer.

There are two forms of marriage: Traditional and statutory. Traditional marriages include a dowry payment to the bride's family. A dowry may include money and the breaking of a kola nut. The sharing and eating of kola nut symbolizes peace and life. There will be also be cultural dancing, singing, and performances by drummers.

A biblical reference for marriage is 1 Corinthians 13:4-8: Love is patient and kind; love does not envy or boast; it is not arrogant or rude. It does not insist on its own way; it is not irritable or resentful; it does not rejoice at wrongdoing but rejoices with the truth. Love bears all things, believes all things, hopes all things, endures all things. Love never ends. As for prophecies, they will pass away; as for tongues, they will cease; as for knowledge, it will pass away.

These couples are modeled and supported by older or similar couples in the communities. These couples share time with new couples via house gatherings and celebrations or house fellowship with many couples. These experiences are very beneficial to the new couples to learn the way of the cross-culture relationship. Some resources that are helpful in learning about the Liberian culture are available at the local library, like articles by the West Africa Magazine, the Liberian Newsletter, and the World Encyclopedia. Another resource is the local embassy that provides information about the land, people, and culture. There are also organizations that work indirectly with volunteers: The Peace Corps, and Crossroads. Volunteers within these organizations have served as teachers, preachers, counselors, and farmers. Some resources where you can acquire information via Friends of Liberia.

The Liberian population is a growing population in the United States of America. Many generations of Liberian-Afro-America families are uniting with other cultures and creating the historical history of Liberia. It has been a mixture of United States and Great Britain, French and other European governments. The first President of Liberia was Joseph Robert. Mr. Robert networked with businessman but encountered many problems. One of President Robert's accomplishments was to establish Liberia as an independent nation. Liberia became a free republic on July 26, 1847. Today many Liberians celebrate that day as Independence Day. This day has come to symbolize of freedom, opportunities for trade and development in the country of Liberia and celebrated around the world.

Liberia is known for its business relationship with the Firestone Tire and Rubber Company (an American company) which strengthens the Liberian economy by providing employment opportunities. Leasing the land brought money in the Liberian Government, and Liberians were invested in the land and borrow monies for other types of businesses. Many of the Liberian celebrations are often commemorative with cultural dancing that is associated with their culture. The dancing is often part of the celebration at events, such as birthdays, weddings, and family graduations. Dancing is often displayed in groups of men and women. Some of the dances are uniform with steps and movements that are taught early on in their development. Women will dance with women, showing unity as a mother, grandmother, aunt, sister and friend. A traditional matrimonial dance is usually performed at wedding receptions where the bride and groom lead the family and friends in a march around the reception hall in a circular formation where individuals place their hands on another person's shoulder and march, sing and strut to African lyrics. Another traditional wedding dance is where family and friends form a circle beginning with the wedding couple in the center to initiate the dance. Then the wedding couple steps out of the circle, and then another man or women enters the circle and performs a dance and the members follow the rhythmic dance. This repeats until everyone has had an opportunity to enter the circle. Other festive dance celebrations are conducted at parties, family gatherings, birthdays and national celebrations. Dancing is a rhythmic motion of Liberian culture displayed in movement to show rejoicing, celebration and love.

African clothing is very festive with vibrant colors that are patriotic to the continent of Africa or that is sentimental to an individual's country flag. There is certain attire that is worn, women tend to wear the Lap-Pa, which is a wrap-around skirt. The fabric is a print of solid color often representing the Kent-Cloth, which is a widely used cloth in West African countries.

Many of the men's attire consist of shirt and pants with a robe. The authentic fabric is often made and designed by Liberian seamstresses and designers. Many of the Liberian seamstresses have learned as children and choose the occupation of a tailor as adults. Some of the tailors prepare and sew school uniforms for the children in the private and public schools located in Liberia.

Western Family Tradition

There is a distinction between the family relationships of Americans and Liberians. In the American tradition, the union of the family is composed if the husband, wife and children. A relationship of acceptance is also formulated between the mother and father of the bride of the American family. Whereas with the Liberian mates, the relationship is composed of the husband, wife, children, grandparents, aunts, nieces, nephews, brothers and sisters. The American bride or groom is marrying into the entire family and in addition, the entire family acceptance is required in the Liberian tradition.

The Liberian extended families will provide outreach services to the American bride or groom in the form of cooking lessons, on how to prepare meals, cleaning, laundry, and cultural celebration preparations of etiquette, on how meals are served for the immediate family or a group of people. The Liberian community is a group of people that are close knit and provide a nurturing system of love and care to the children and acceptance of the American bride and groom's families.

Liberians are very disciplined people. They stress discipline in the family, early in the developmental stages of the children, where their form of discipline is the traditional force, with a rod or belt. There is no tolerance for disobedience; children are taught at an early age to be respectful to their parents, elders, adults and other significant others. The American bride or groom adopts and incorporates their form of discipline in raising their children. Some lessons of discipline are often taught with discussion with the child the behavior, that is inappropriate, punishment, restricted activities, and the rod or belt.

The Liberian families are very friendly and giving. Liberians often have a southern hospitality of opening up their homes for friends and family members. The American bride and groom must adapt to home visitors coming to their homes. Liberian's homes are always available for sisters, brothers, mothers and fathers to visit for a short or long duration with the bride and groom. For the American bride and groom it can be an adjustment, physically, emotionally, and psychologically. For the Liberians it is a cultural custom to provide housing and food to families and friends at any time. There is no disruption for a Liberian in lifestyle, because the motto, "it takes a whole village, united to raise a child," literally the children are raised in homes with extended family members and friends.

The Liberian community strives as one which means that the members of the family have regular duties, such as taking care of the home and farm. It is imperative to work as a team in the advancement of the Liberian today for the development of the country.

There are many Americo-Liberians who choose to reside in Liberia. This decision is a mutual decision between the man and wife. It is an adjustment for the American to sacrifice and adopt the Liberian culture. Many America-Liberians have lived in Liberia and the Americans have adjusted well. The elders in their community have a role model, a teacher and an adoptive mother and father. The

American is treated just as a Liberian, she has the same duties as the village woman; to cook, to clean, and to take care of the children and her husband. The adjustment for the women is adjusting to the ways and customs of West Africa. Liberians will welcome Americans into their families, work force, and in addition, an opportunity to purchase land while married to a Liberian. The children have the opportunity and legal right to own land and start their own business.

Liberian artifacts are hand carved from wood, ivory, and mahogany are often made by members of certain tribes. Many of the sculptures will represent women with child; symbolizing fertility, and man as elderly; symbolizing wisdom and head of the household. Many of the carvings of the animals are detailed; animals that are often made as sculptures are deer and their antlers, lion, giraffe, zebra, elephants. There are also some symbols made into carvings that represent love, marriage, female and male, and the country.

Many of the women, men and children will shop at the market. The marketplace is where individuals and families can purchase groceries such as rice, meats, and vegetables such as Cassava, Bitter Cola, Julep Leaves, Palm Butter, Fufu and Plantain flour. The marketplace is where families gather seven days a week to purchase groceries to feed their families. It is very common for multiple families to share purchasing groceries, especially if they live in the same village.

The motto, "it takes a whole village to feed a family," applies to Liberian communities. Many families are able to survive both financially and economically. Other items can be purchased from the market like artifacts, gold, silver, material, handbags and wooden carvings and picture art frames.

Family history associated with tribal warfare has often caused family disputes over ownership of property, gold, silver and politics. Liberia is a beautiful country that is near the water with many beaches. The division that has occurred in the country begins with tribal control in the politics, religion, and culture. The country has been in constant warfare among their own people since the time of Samuel Doe's Leadership. With a history of the unfair political elections of former presidents, they have stirred up animosity, hatred and division. Often, many who are in control have dominated the villages, homes, and communities without permission.

Liberia has suffered in resources, growth, and development as a nation. The country has often been divided by religion, tribes and political ties. This is a year of celebration and history as the people of Liberia have voted for the first woman President, Mrs. Ellen Johnson Sir Leaf who won the election fairly. The country prepared for the inauguration of the first woman President to take office in January of 2006.

A unique custom of Liberians is the greeting which is often in the form of embracing each other, with a hug, kiss, or handshake. When two women embrace each other, it is with a hug and a kiss, or a handshake.

The Liberian handshake is a very unique greeting, which is offered when first meeting with another person, or to show camaraderie, friendship and love. The right hand is extended to the left hand; the thumb and the third fingers grasp, and then both hands are released (shown in image). The handshake is a sign of true friendship. If the handshake is extended twice, then that is an indication of best friends. The handshake is formally done with the men only (as seen in image).

Tribal marks are often displayed on men and women to distinguish ancestry tribal relations. Some marks are located on the face, hands, and bodies, often in the form of a tattoo mark. All tribal marks represent a history of their heritage.

Tie-dye indigo is a form of art work that is often designed in the clothing or fabrics. The cloth is often tied in a formation of knots, then it is dipped into the dye with one color or several colors to create a pattern design on the cloth. Once the cloth has dried it can be used to make lapels, pants, and dresses.

Musical Instruments: The musical rhymes and songs have both an African and mixture of both Caribbean and Spanish descent. Some of the instruments that are used are drums, banjos, string instruments, and maracas with beads. Most of the instruments are handmade from resources within their villages such as wood, leathers, string and iron.

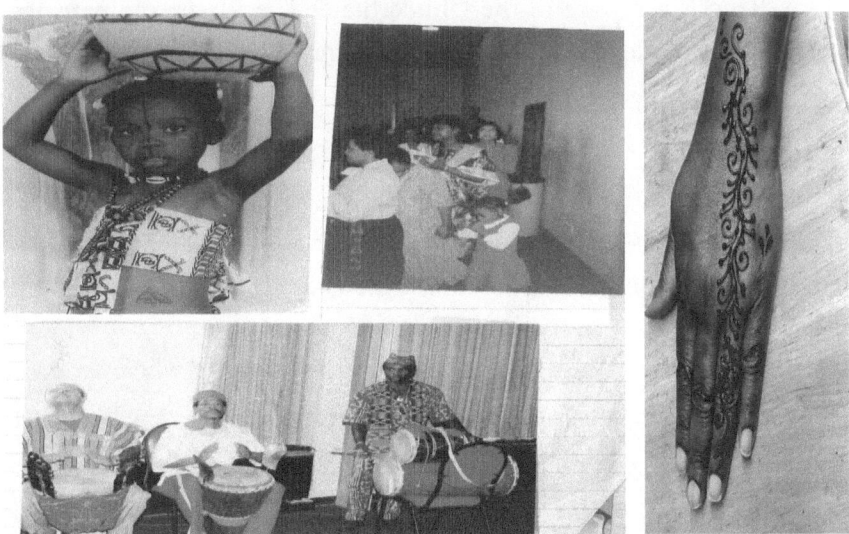

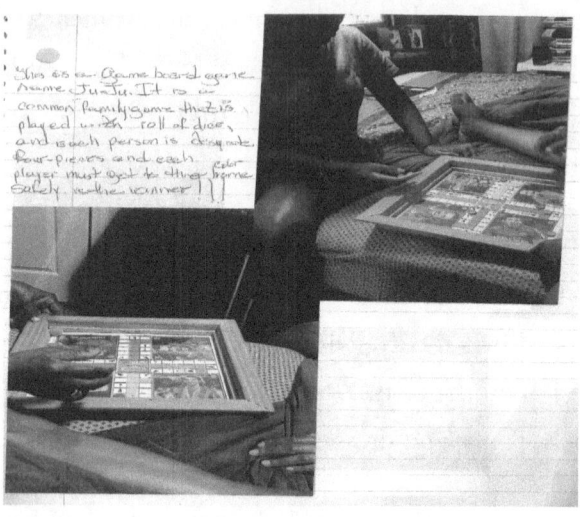

Jewelry: Liberian jewelry is in the form of gold and silver. The traditional ring is the V-Ring. It is very unique in that it is the form of a v-shape, and is often a fashionable ring for Liberian women. Some women will have their wedding rings made in the shape of a v. The V-Ring is very rare in the United States. Necklaces and earrings are often made out of 14-karat gold or 20-karat gold and uniquely designed. Some of the jewelry is made out of ivory.

Shoes: Some of the shoes are made out of snakeskins and are often designed to match their outfits. Some of the men's sandals are handmade out of leather, often in a shape of a flip-flop.

Hair braiding is very unique in the Liberian culture, where women will corn roll each other's hair. It is often referred as a French-handed corn rolls. These corn rolls can be done in many sizes and lengths.

There are many styles to choose among, as you can add hair to accentuate length and style. This form of braiding usually takes about two to three hours. Another form of braiding that is common in

Liberia is single braids, where hair is added to your hair for length and style. This form of braiding usually takes about six to eight hours to complete. Hair braiding is taught very young to the girls; by the age of twelve, a young girl can successfully braid and corn roll hair.

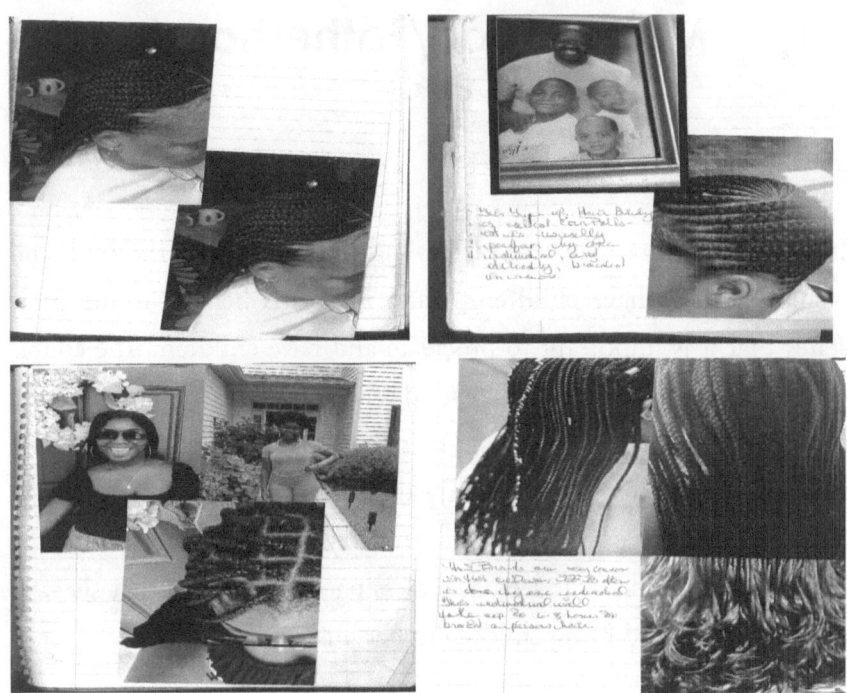

Many Liberian women will wear a scarf or cloth that completely covers their hair but is designed in a fashionable style that will coordinate with the dress clothing they are wearing. It is common to wear a matching hair scarf with a formal dress or lappa to a formal affair such as weddings, church, dinners and family celebrations. Many of the clothing designed today will have the matching scarf to wear.

Motherhood/Fatherhood

In African culture it is very sacred and important that the man and woman plan to have children. Many Liberians believe as the Bible states that it is important to procreate and have children. The couple believes that they are blessed by God when children are born into the family. If a woman bears a son, it is seen that the family name and heritage will carry over into the next generation. This will make the father of the child proud that his ancestry will continue. As for the birth of a girl child, it is seen as a blessing to the family that she will one day marry and bring children to her husband's family.

A traditional ritual is that children as babies are often transported by their mother on their back wrapped with Kente-cloth and carried within the home as well as outside the home. This is often initiated because the mother will need to complete household chores and complete errands to the market for food. Like the American culture, children are often transported in strollers. When a child is born into the Liberian community, it is the husband's Mother that will sacrifice six months to a year to come and take care of the child.

Baby christenings are an interval service of the growth and development for children. Liberians view the birth of a child as a blessing from God. The ritual for a child born is after thirty days, the baby is introduced to the elders, family and friends in a formal ceremony that is often hosted in the parent's home or church. A sacred ceremony is held with the blessings of the parents, God, and church family and friends. During this sacred ceremony, fruit is offered to the congregation, which symbolizes unity, and represents the bitter and the good that life has to offer. Celebration of music and movement offers praises to God for the birth of a new child in the community. All members invited to the celebration will dance around the child to show unity. While dancing, members of the family, friends, and congregation will celebrate by contributing monies to the child, as the child is located in the center of the floor. This is a community collection to give to the child to start a savings account. Also, at the ceremony there are blessings bestowed upon the family from the parents, godparents and the community village. It is often said, "It takes a whole village to raise a child."

The traditional ceremonials associated with the birth of children are christenings and baptism. The traditional Naming Ceremony has an order of service that is affiliated with a musical prelude. This can be in the form of songs or musical instruments. The next witnessing of the talking drum- which will call on the ancestors to bless the occasion.

Procession- the family comes out: Mother, father, child/children and godparents.

Scripture Readings: Psalm 23 and Luke 2:21-24.

Breaking of the fruit- this symbolizes the friendship and fellowship (fruit can be an orange).

Minister or Elder- In the breaking of this fruit, we call on you to join us in praising God and celebrating this gift of life.

Congregation- God, our Father, God, our Mother, God who gave this child to us, we fall on our knees and pray for you. Bless this child whom we name today.

Playing of the drums- Talking drum will call on the ancestors to bless the family.

Parent- As God has given to us, we give to you, to share, to protect, to parent and to love.

Presentation of the child- God has given us this gift to nurture, love, protect and instruct. We present this child to the community.

Congregation- O, God, help us to be worthy of the children you have entrusted to our care and grant us strength to fulfill our commitment to this child.

Receiving of the child- Godparents, we receive this gift of God and present him to the world. May God guide his steps and protect his life.

Congregation- May God guides his steps and protects his life. God grant us strength to fulfill our commitments and make us worthy of the children you have entrusted to our care.

Talking Drum- will call on the ancestors to bless this child.

Lifting of the child- Father, we lift you to your greatest height. Between you and God there is no limit to your potential. You must be like nobody else except what God wants you to be. Always strive to be the best you can be.

The sprinkling of water symbolizes parental authority and as your caretaker we know you will follow what we, your parents, will teach you to do.

Musical selection
Naming of the child
Minister: What shall we name this child?
Response: Mother and Father whispering the name in his ear.
Prayer of dedication.
Selection
Blessings of the Elders
Presentation of gifts
Family friends
The Family
The Community
Community Dance
Benediction
Refreshments

This Program can be altered to serve the needs of the families who are having the Naming Ceremony or Christening.

The Baptismal Ceremony:

Matthew 28: 18-20; Romans 6:3-11

According to the New National Baptist Bible

In addition, Jesus came and spoke unto them, saying, "All power is given unto me in heaven and in earth. Go ye therefore, and teach all nations, baptizing them in the name of the Father, and of the Son, and of the Holy Ghost."

Teaching them to observe all things whatsoever I have commanded you: and lord, I am with you always, even unto the end of the world.

Know ye not, that so many of us as were baptized into Jesus Christ were baptized into his death?

Therefore, we are buried with him by baptism into death: that just as Christ was raised up from the dead by the glory of the Father, even so we also should walk in newness of life.

For if we have been planted together in the likeness of his resurrection:

Knowing this, that the old man is crucified with him, that the body of sin might be destroyed, that henceforth we should not serve sin.

For he that is dead is freed from sin.

Now if we were dead with Christ, we believe that we shall also live with him.

Knowing that Christ being raised from the dead dieth no more; death hath no more dominion over him.

For in that he died, he died unto sin once: but in that he liveth he liveth unto God.

Likewise, reckon ye also yourselves to be dead indeed unto sin, but alive unto God through Jesus Christ our Lord.

The Catholic Blessings Ceremonies

According to the archdioceses

Act 2: 38, Matthew 19:14

For the Catholic faith, baptism is a sacrament of initiation into the life of children of God. Baptism is literally and symbolically not only cleansing, but also dying and rising again with Christ. Catholics believe that baptism is necessary for the cleansing of the taint of original sin, and for that reason infant baptism is a common practice. Having been baptizing in the Catholic Church allows entry into the church and access to all of the rights and responsibilities as full members, and access to the Holy Communion.

The services rendered in the Catholic Church are similar to the Christians with the expectation that the child is sprinkled with water over the head (aspersion), or pouring water over the head (affusion). The priest officiates in the presence of the parents, godparents, and friends. It is required in order to serve as godparents that the parents are both of the Catholic faith (preferred) to receive the child as their own. Catholics baptize in the name of the Father, of the Son, and of the Holy Spirit- not three Gods, but one God subsisting in three persons.

After the formal baptism, the priest provides communion for family and friends in celebration that the child is now blessed. These forms of baptism are always held in a Catholic Church and if a church is not available, the priest must make the accommodations within the villages.

History

Liberia is located in West Africa. Neighboring countries are Sierra Leon, and the Ivory Coast. The capital of Liberia is Monrovia, named after former president James Monroe. The total landmass is estimated about 99,067 square kilometers. The climate is tropical, with rainy seasons and hot weather. The economy is agriculture based consisting of palm oil and kernels, sweet potatoes, plantains, sugar cane, rice, cassava, and rubber. The industries are iron-ore, timber, rubber, and wood.

Liberia Sande'/Poro Society
Traditional Society

Liberia has sixteen major tribes, they are culturally linked, especially those that members of the Poro and Sande' societies.

The Poro is a traditional sacred society for men. The Sande' society is for the women. Traditional sacred rites are administered by these societies to boys and girls by the chief Zoes in a special location where the initiation rites are performed.

The Non-Pro/Sande' tribes are:

A. Gio

B. Grebo

C. Kru

D. Khran

E. Sarpoe

F. Mandingo

Those of the Poro/Sande' Societies are:

A. Bassa

B. Gbandi

C. Gola

D. Dey

E. Loma

F. Kpelleh

G. Kissi

H. Mano

I. Vai

J. Gbellah

Those of the Poro/Sande' are traditional bush (forest) institutions where boys and girls are trained in the social and educational aspects culturally- each tribe has its or a collective institution where the sacred rites are learned and performed.

The men are educated amongst other things to:

A. Take care of a family- providing protection, etc.

B. Prepare palm oil and other useful money (economic) ventures, plotting of mats, making and beating the drums, and creative crafts.

C. Be courteous to elders, farming as farming-as a means of finding food to sustain the family amongst other useful trainings.

The females are taught how to:

A. Respect their husbands and elders in the society.
B. Take care of their children and family members.
C. Prepare food- including farming, fishing and the undertaking of basic household activities.
D. Traditional weaving- baskets, sasas, fishing nets, etc.

Traditional Marriage

This form of marriage is unlike the Western, which is performed in:

A. Church- Officiated by a Priest/Pastor.
B. Court- Confirmation of marriage by a judge.

Interestingly, the association of Liberian Female Lawyers has seen the need to propose for Legislation:

A. That a female married traditionally should enjoy inheritance rights of the husband's property or properties.
B. If not the property of the family, that in the event that husband has expired, the wife goes to a selected family member, preferably a brother. However, the wife has the option to choose another Liberian male in the family or outside the family and remarry.
C. The children of traditional marriages are entitled to some benefit of the expired father.
D. The wife may choose either in the family, which is not compulsory or at her own choosing.

The traditional ceremonies for women wedding celebrations in both America and Liberia have many similarities beginning with the wedding shower. The bride to be invites many of her friends, colleagues, and family relatives (a formal invitation is mailed out with a date, time and location of the shower).

As an invited guest, individuals would shower the bride with gifts for the house and items for herself. This is a celebration of women, usually given or sponsored by women in wisdom, faith and fellowship. The gifts that are usually given are lingerie for the bride-to-be, or household items for both the bride and groom such as a blender, microwave, china, drinking glasses, and silverware. There is also an abundance of cultural foods served such as Jolliff-Rice, Cassava Leaf, fried chicken and fried plantain, punch or ginger-beer.

The traditional ceremonies for the men wedding celebrations in both America and Liberia are similar: such as the Groom-to-be, "the invitation is extended to male-only, where men will gather together, friends and other male relatives in celebration of marriage and future fatherhood. On some occasion food is also served similar menu as the shower for the women: Plava sauce with rice, Jollific rice and friend chicken. It is often that the men will give a monetary contribution to the groom-to-be.

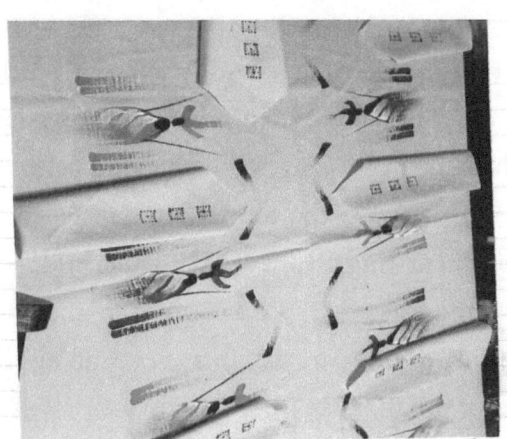

The Table Cloth is hand made, hand Paint, representation of Village with the women gathering and preparing the meals The Table clothes are usually used for special celebrations such as birthdays, Holidays and Family social events.

Engagements

This is a joint celebration between the families of the partners-to-be. This is a formal or informal gathering of friends and family in the announcing of their intent to marry. Dancing and celebration with food and drink. At this event, the formal announcement and presentation of an engagement ring is presented to the bride-to-be. Both families are present and exchange speeches given by the groom-to-be's parents and the bride-to-be's parents. This event can also have the blessing of a minister or priest.

Liberian Songs, Music, Drums & Folklores

The Liberians have always traditionally celebrated with the songs that are patriotic to the country of Liberia; "All Hail Liberia", "Hail", and "All Hail Liberia Hail." These songs are sung to pay homage and honor to any formal program or incurrence in the recognition of Independence Day celebrated every July 26th, which is the anniversary of the founding of the country. Liberians sing this song proudly in recognition of the birth of their country.

Some songs are sung traditionally at religious events like, "Lift Jesus higher- Lower, lower, lift Jesus lower, lower." Another favorite song is, "Aboni-a"- 'Aboni-a, Oh, Aboni-abonia. Jesus is the light of the world." These among other songs are traditional and are sung at social events and gatherings such as christenings, funerals, weddings, graduations, family reunions and inaugurations. In the villages with some of the tribes, these songs are sung while in the garden, cutting plants, fishing and sewing.

The drums known as the talking drums are a form of communication in both the villages of Liberia to the homes of Liberians in the United States. Some of the drums are shaped like an hourglass, and made out of wood, with cow or snakeskin covering both ends of the drums. The drums can communicate messages of peace and warnings of danger, joy and love in the communities of the Liberians.

Other instruments that are used are xylophones, bells, horns, clappers and other string instruments, guitars and string harps. Many of these instruments are hand carved wood from the trees in the villages.

The Liberian music is a mixture of West African rhythms, West Indian Calypso, Latin American rhythms and South African tunes. The music is often played at funerals, wedding receptions, baby showers, dances, and family gatherings.

Funerals

Liberian family traditions concerning the loss of a loved one are that the families, friends and neighbors will come together and help the family in need. The help will consist of preparing food to assist financially with the cost of burying the loved one. It is also customary that the family will have a traditional ceremony at a local church and the repast at the family's home. This celebration of life of the loved one will be shared with friends and family members at the home. A feast of food will be provided, and the gathering will occur for 12-24 hours. After this time, the immediate family may mourn the loss of the loved one for six months to a year. It is traditional for the family to wear something black to show that they are in the mourning period. This allows the family to pay respect and the grieving period is less traumatic on the family.

The elders in the Liberian community often share folklores and folk tales. It tells a story to the children in the villages, or within the family. Many lessons are learning from these stories such as: wisdom, love, success and peace. "It is often the words of the elders that foster the growth and development of the children in the villages."

The Seeds We Sowed

Poem by: Umvalli Lowenthal

Many years ago back in our native land, in the little mining town, at the foot of old mount Nimbe our tender seeds of love we sowed. In our youthful hearts, these seeds of love, we sowed for eternity. However, this we did not know, till destiny came our way. For the many years past, along the banks of the rivers of our hearts, our seeds of love sowed many years ago, continue to be nurture unbeknown to us. With fate taking its toll, in a foreign land, our seeds have come to sprout. However, unlike our little mining town, this soil has not the anchor for our sprouting seeds.

So from God, wisdom we must seek from the ancestors, our culture we must seize; and from our hosts in this land of exile, knowledge we must acquire to assure, that the seeds we sowed will germinate and flourish. If the tender seeds we sowed at the foot of old mount Nimba must bloom. In addition, bear fruits in this land of exile we must stand firm on the banks of the river of sincerity and invoke the spirit of divine love.

If the seeds of love we sowed many years ago, in that little mining town in our native land should take root beside the river of harmony o'how our thirst for the love we have lost will be quenched from the fountain of joy. Our sprouted seeds shall reveal to us.

National Anthem of Liberia, West Africa

"All hail, Liberia Hail! All hail Liberia Hail! This glorious land of liberty shall long be ours; though new her name, green be her fame, and mighty be her powers...in joy and gladness with our hearts untied, we'll shout the freedom of a race benighted, long live Liberia, happy land, a home of glorious liberty by God's command.

All hail, Liberia hail! All hail, Liberia Hail! In union strong success is sure, we cannot fail, with God above our rights to prove, we will o'er all prevail, with heart and hand our country's cause defending, we'll meet the foe with valor unpretending, long live Liberia, happy land, a home of glorious liberty by God's command."

This is the national anthem that is sung by all Liberians, America-Liberians, and cross-cultural Liberians unite as in one accord both in the United States, Europe, and Liberia and Africa. Arms are united around the world, and the marks of peace are permeating around all. As children, the Liberians are taught the National Anthem, likewise as the American children are taught the United States of America National Anthem. These two anthems are shared mutually and respected at both American and Liberian programs.

Immigration

Many of the Liberians are migrating to the United States and Europe because of the opportunities in education. Many Liberians will come into the U.S. with a student visa passport. This passport enables Liberians to study at a local university and obtain the following degrees: Bachelor of Arts, Masters and Ph.D. degrees. Upon completion of their educational quest, many Liberians will marry in the U.S. and return home (Liberia or remain in the U.S.). While other Liberians come to the states on a visitor's visa. These Liberians are often visiting family members who reside in the states or Europe or another African country. Some Liberians choose to extend their visitor's pass from three months to one year.

Some other Liberians who have entered into the United States for school decide to remain there and choose to become an American Citizen. As an American Citizen, Liberians have all the rights as citizens. Some Liberians choose to have dual citizenship, and they remain both a citizen in the U.S. and in their home country of Liberia.

There are some Liberians who have applied for political asylum. These Liberians have fled the country due to the war or political ties, or a coupe. These Liberians do not have permission to return to their homeland. Many of these Liberians will continue to reside in other African countries, Europe, or the United States. Having political asylum, many Liberians have as many rights as those Liberians who possess a green card in the U.S. The only exception is they are unable to vote in elections.

Process for applying for a Green Card

When applying for a Green Card here in the U.S., Liberians married to Americans must be married at least six months to two years before applying. The procedure involves planning a visit to the local immigration office where the couple resides and presenting the following documents: Social Security Card, Birth Certificate, and Marriage Certificate. At some locations a picture of both mates are required. After the documents have been submitted then the Green Card should be in the mail 4-6 weeks. The Green Card allows persons from other countries to be able to work in the country they are residing in. This document is important to employers because persons from other countries must have a Green Card for employment.

With the new President Ellen Johnson Sir Leaf, newly appointed President by Free Republic of Liberia citizens. The President's goals were to establish harmony and peace in the country. President Johnson's goal was to create a country where fellow Liberians can return home and contribute their talent, education and support to the rebuilding of Liberia. Many Liberians are truly excited about the reconciliation and rebuilding initiative of the country of Liberia.

President Ellen Johnson Sir Leaf returns to Liberia as the 23rd President, native of Monrovia, Liberia. She received her early education at the College of West Africa, in Monrovia achieving a BA in Accounting at Madison Business College in Madison Wisconsin and an economics diploma from the University of Colorado. She also has extensive experience in Business, Finance, and Management, and is a graduate of Harvard University. She is a mother of four sons, and six grand children. She has a repertoire of work experience, beginning with serving as the President of the Liberian Bank for Development and Investment. She has served as the Senior Loan Officer for the World Bank in Washington, D.C. She is the founder and CEO of Kormah Development Corporation and founder of Measuagon, a non-profit organization supporting community development in Liberia.

Organizations like Licore- Liberians interested in reconciliation and settlement established in Washington D.C., to help Liberians both here in the U.S. and in Liberia. A man started this organization named Jim who envisioned Liberians here in Washington D.C. coming together to aid the needs of the Liberians here in the states. After the death of Jim, Mr. Justus Y. Reeves became CEO of Licore. During his leadership, he envisioned providing resources for Liberians abroad and within the states. Collaborating with Friends of Liberia, Ellen Johnson Sir Leaf volunteer and other organizations to reach peaceful relationships with the various Liberian tribes. Licore assisted referrals for food programs, assistance with applying for a Green card, assistance with housing, and educational applications for GED and college. Assistance to various missionaries in preparation for traveling to Liberia, and helping Liberians. This organization provided services for five consecutive years, and since that time, there has not been another company to provide those resources to the needs of Liberians.

It is hopeful that under the leadership of Ellen Johnson Sir Leaf that many programs will be reinstated both here in the states and Liberia. It will take both efforts of Liberians working in the States and Liberia to be the country it is blessed to be. The former President had created positive relationships with the United States and other African countries. The Nigerian government has been very instrumental in building strong bonds of friendship, heritage and leadership with the Liberian government. "President Ellen Johnson Sir Leaf envisions a renewal of Liberia, which encompasses a new political order, a new social order, and a new economical order." She hopes to achieve the following changes: constitutional reform, land reform, judicial reform, civil service reform and decentralization of power during her six term year as the President of Liberia. Many Liberians have a lot of love and respect for the "Iron Lady that has returned to serve her people."

The current President of Liberia is George Weah. He is the twenty-fifth president. He is a renowned sports figure and received many notable awards for his accomplishments. As the rising president of Liberia he has been able to negotiate to strengthen the infrastructure of Liberia which will aid in the economic development of the country. He is an inspirational visionary of hope and aspires to raise the healthy birth rate by building maternity clinics and medical clinics, promoting education, and increasing housing options.

The Vice President of Liberia is Jewel Taylor. She is a strong advocate of women's rights and health as well as children's welfare.

www.ingramcontent.com/pod-product-compliance
Lightning Source LLC
Chambersburg PA
CBHW061222280526
45784CB00006B/2595